W9-CIK-193

Biking

Paul Mason

A⁺

Smart Apple Media

Smart Apple Media
2140 Howard Drive West
North Mankato, Minnesota 56003

First published in 2007 by
MACMILLAN EDUCATION AUSTRALIA PTY LTD
627 Chapel Street, South Yarra, Australia 3141

Visit our Web site at www.macmillan.com.au or go directly to www.macmillanlibrary.com.au

Associated companies and representatives throughout the world.

Library of Congress Cataloging-in-Publication Data

Mason, Paul, 1967-
    Biking / by Paul Mason.
    p. cm. — (Recreational sports)
    Includes index.
    ISBN 978-1-59920-130-6
    1. Cycling—Juvenile literature. I. Title.

    GV1043.5.M35 2007
    796.6—dc22

                                                    2007004594

Edited by Vanessa Lanaway
Text and cover design by Pier Vido
Page layout by Pier Vido
Photo research by Naomi Parker
Illustrations by Boris Silvestri
Map on pp. 28–9 by Pier Vido

Printed in U.S.

Acknowledgements
The author and the publisher are grateful to the following for permission to reproduce
copyright material:

Front cover photograph: BMX rider jumping, courtesy of P&S Images/Photolibrary.

Photos courtesy of:
Duomo/Corbis/Australian Picture Library, p. 21; Chase Jarvis/Corbis/Australian Picture
Library, p. 20; Digital Stock/Corbis, p. 13; Ty Allison/Getty Images, p. 18; Harald Eisenberger/
Getty Images, p. 4; John Kelly/Getty Images, p. 30; Stefan Schuetz/Getty Images, p. 26; Henrik
Sorensen/Getty Images, p. 25; Istockphoto, p. 14; Anzeletti/Istockphoto, p. 16; Sue McDonald/
Istockphoto, pp. 5, 10 (top); Millanovic/Istockphoto, p. 27 (bottom); Maxim Petrichuk/
Istockphoto, p. 11; Jon Rasmussen/Istockphoto, p. 24; Jennifer Trenchard/Istockphoto, p. 27
(top); Evan Jeffery www.evanjeffery.com.au, p. 9; Paul Mason, p. 6; Claire Francis/MEA Photos,
pp. 10 (bottom), 12; PhotoDisc, p. 17; Chase Jarvis/Photolibrary, p. 7; P&S Images/Photolibrary,
pp. 1, 22; Photos.com, p. 8.

While every care has been taken to trace and acknowledge copyright, the publisher tenders
their apologies for any accidental infringement where copyright has proved untraceable.
Where the attempt has been unsuccessful, the publisher welcomes information that would
redress the situation.

Please note
At the time of printing, the Internet addresses appearing in this book were correct. However,
because of the dynamic nature of the Internet, we cannot guarantee that all Web addresses
will remain correct.

Contents

Glossary words

When a word is printed in **bold**, you can look up its meaning in the glossary on page 31.

Recreational sports

Recreational sports are the activities we do in our spare time. These are sports that people do for fun, not necessarily for competition.

You have probably tried some recreational sports already. Maybe you would like to know more about them or find out about new ones? Try as many as you can—not just biking. Also try hiking, fishing, kayaking, climbing, and snorkeling. This will help you find one you really love doing.

Benefits of sports

Recreational sports are lots of fun but they also have other benefits. People who exercise regularly are usually healthier. They find it easier to concentrate and do better in school or at work.

"Nothing compares to the simple pleasure of a bike ride."

U.S. President John F. Kennedy

Riding a bike is a fun way to exercise.

Biking

Once you can ride a bike, there are many things you can use it for. You can ride to your friends' houses or to school. You could ride a mountain bike down an exciting downhill course. Or you might learn **BMX** tricks that will amaze and impress your friends.

Bikes are really useful. They can go almost anywhere. Bikes rarely get caught in traffic jams. They are easy to park and inexpensive to own.

Almost anyone can ride a bike. Many people who begin biking when they are young never stop. Some are still pedaling when they are eighty or ninety years old.

BMXs are great in the city or town, where there are lots of opportunities to do tricks.

WATCH OUT!

Wear safety gear for cycling. Helmets and gloves protect your head and hands. Some riders even wear padding and motocross body armor as well.

Getting started

There are lots of different kinds of bikes—**racers**, BMXs, **mountain bikes**, and even folding bikes. There are so many choices.

Choosing a bike

There is no kind of bike that is best. However, a mountain bike is good for beginners because it will let them try lots of different kinds of biking, such as:

- city cycling
- cross-country riding
- downhill riding
- doing tricks
- long-distance rides on- or off-road.

Mountain bikes can be cheaply bought in second-hand stores. If you buy a second-hand bike, take someone with you who can check that everything works well.

lightweight frame makes cycling easier

front suspension absorbs bumps

Mountain bikes can be ridden on-road and off-road.

tire treads grip wet or muddy ground

Off-road cycling

Mountain bikes are great for riding on off-road routes. They usually have **suspension**, which makes it more comfortable to ride over bumps. Some mountain bikes have suspension for both wheels.

Road riding

Cycling on the road can be dangerous because of the traffic on busy roads. It is important to learn the rules for safe cycling. Keep alert to danger and use bicycle paths whenever possible. And always wear a helmet.

"Now that's something that makes life worth living!"

famous writer Jack London talking about cycling.

When cycling on the road, use the bicycle lane whenever possible.

7

Setting up your bike

Setting up your bike means adjusting the saddle and handlebars so that you have a good riding position. This makes your bike faster and easier to ride.

The frame

A bike's frame is made of metal tubes. The back wheel, pedals, saddle, handlebars, and **forks** are attached to the frame. You need a frame that you can comfortably stand over with both feet on the ground. As long as the frame is the right size, you will be able to adjust all the other parts of the bike to suit you.

Adjusting your bike

How you set up your bike depends on what kind of riding you do. BMX riders and downhill riders prefer lower saddles. So do beginners. Road racers sometimes set the saddle very high.

Top tip!

If your riding position feels uncomfortable at first, begin with the saddle set lower.

A good riding position such as this one should be comfortable and make your bike easy to ride.

Basic setup

Follow this step-by-step guide to find a basic setup for your bike. You can then adjust the height of the seat to suit your own style of riding.

1 Handlebars
Handlebars should be set at the same height as the saddle, or a little higher.

2 The right size frame
You need a one- to four-inch (3-10 cm) gap between this tube and your body when you stand over the bike.

3 Saddle angle
Use a level to make sure the saddle is level with the ground.

4 Saddle height
When you sit on the saddle with your heel on the pedal at its lowest point, your leg should be nearly straight.

Adjust the setup of your bike to suit you.

WATCH OUT!

Make sure all the bolts on your bike are tightened after you have finished making adjustments.

Bike maintenance

Being able to do some basic maintenance is important for any cyclist. It means they are able to keep their bike running smoothly and safely.

Regular checks

Every biker needs to do regular checks to make sure their bike is safe to ride. Brakes, **gears**, and forks are among the most important things to check.

Gears

Do the gears change smoothly, and does the bike stay in gear properly? If not, they need adjustment before you ride.

Make sure your brakes work properly before tackling a slope like this one.

WATCH OUT!

If you cannot fix a problem yourself, make sure someone else does. Otherwise, your bike could be dangerous to ride.

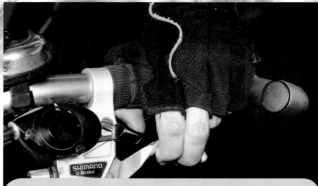

There should always be plenty of space between the brake lever and the handlebars when you put the brakes on.

Brakes

Check that the brakes work smoothly and stop the bike quickly. If not, do not ride until they have been adjusted.

Forks

Check that the forks are secure by gripping the front wheel between your knees, then rocking the handlebars back and forth. If there is any movement or clicking, they need to be adjusted. Another sign that the forks are loose is a knocking feeling when you brake hard.

Check that your brakes work perfectly before riding.

 **Top tip!**

Use these tips to identify common problems with your bike.

Problem	Cause
squeaky brakes	**brake pads** are not lined up or wheel rims are dirty
squeaking noise while pedaling	chain needs lubrication
clicking noise while pedaling	**cranks** are loose
steering wobbly around corners	tires need more air in them

Biking equipment

The only equipment you really need for cycling is a bike and a helmet. But there is a lot of extra equipment you can get to make life on your bike more comfortable.

Water

Make sure you have plenty to drink while out on your bike. Most people carry water in a bottle attached to the frame. You can also buy special water-carrying backpacks. Either of these things makes it easier to take a drink while you are cycling.

Tool kits

Many riders carry a small tool kit with them, especially if they are going off-road. Even having the tools for mending a **puncture** can turn out to be really useful.

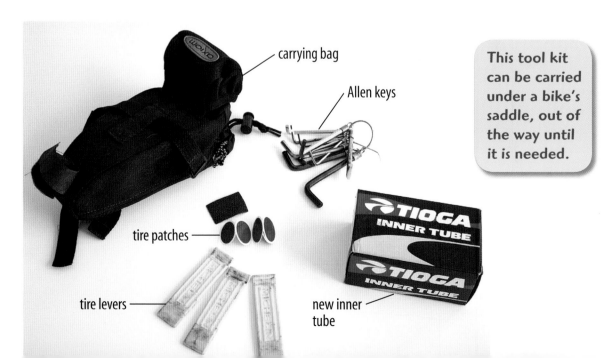

carrying bag

Allen keys

tire patches

tire levers

new inner tube

> This tool kit can be carried under a bike's saddle, out of the way until it is needed.

Clothing

It is important for your bike-riding clothes to be comfortable. Make sure they will keep you warm if it is cold outside or cool if it is hot and sunny. Clothes that are baggy are not great for cycling. Baggy pants can get caught in the chain.

cycling glasses protect the rider's eyes

helmet

fingerless gloves cushion the rider's hands

backpack with water container inside

stretchy top

stretchy shorts with special padding where they touch the saddle

special shoes for cycling

The correct biking equipment will make a ride more comfortable.

Basic skills

One of the key cycling skills is controlling your pedaling speed. Being in the right gear allows you to ride faster and use less energy.

Pedaling speed

Most cyclists aim for a pedaling speed of two downward pushes per second, one on each pedal. The speed at which you can pedal is controlled by your choice of gear. You can only pedal at a comfortable rate if you are in the right gear. Here are some tips.

- If you start bouncing up and down in the saddle, you are in a gear that is too easy. Change down.
- If your body starts rocking up and down or from side to side, you are in a gear that is too hard. Change up.

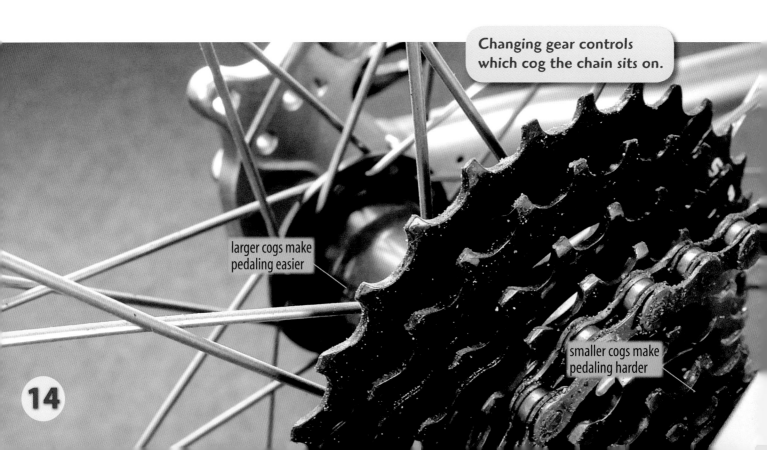

Changing gear controls which cog the chain sits on.

larger cogs make pedaling easier

smaller cogs make pedaling harder

Mending a puncture

One thing all cyclists need to be able to do is mend a puncture. Everybody gets punctures. They usually happen a long way from home or when you are late.

1 Make sure you are in a safe place, away from traffic. Remove the wheel.

2 If the valve is held in place by a nut, undo the nut. Use tire levers to lift the tire from the rim all the way around on one side.

3 Take the inner tube out.

4 Check inside the tire for glass or sharp stones poking through. Remove them if you find any.

5 Blow up the inner tube to find the hole in it.

6 Patch the hole, then blow up the inner tube slightly.

7 Re-fit the inner tube.

8 Put the loose side of the tire back onto the rim and blow it up.

Riding uphill

Many of cyclists find riding uphill very hard work. They do not like fighting the force of **gravity**, and only ride uphill for the pleasure of coming back down again.

With a bit of practice, most people can ride up almost any slope they could walk up. Two things can make cycling uphill much easier.

Pedaling speed

Keeping a good pedaling speed is especially important when riding uphill. Most riders want to pedal quickly, but not too fast. You know you are pedaling too fast if you start to bounce in the saddle.

Weight forward

Keeping your weight forward helps make riding uphill easier. Bend forward and lean toward the handlebars. Try to keep your body still as well. If the bike rocks from side to side, it will not climb as well.

Keeping your weight forward can make riding uphill much easier.

Technique
Riding uphill

Try this technique on a hill you have ridden on before. See how much faster you get to the top.

1 As the slope begins, change down a gear and lean forward slightly.

2 As the climb becomes steeper, bend your elbows, tuck them in, and lean forward more.

3 Change to an easier gear if necessary. You need to be able to keep pedaling smoothly.

4 Keep your body still and your weight on the saddle. Do not stand up on the pedals.

WATCH OUT!
Never stand up on the pedals for long while riding uphill. Change down a gear instead.

Downhill riding

Downhill riding is one of the most thrilling kinds of cycling. In mountain biking, the top racers reach speeds of more than 50 miles (80 km) per hour.

It is important to wear appropriate safety gear when you try downhill riding.

Downhill racers

The ultimate downhill speedsters are downhill mountain bikers. They are not only good at cycling downhill quickly. They are also experts at avoiding rocks, roots, trees, and other obstacles along the course.

Avoiding obstacles

Obstacles such as tree roots, rocks, and holes in the trail sometimes get in your way. There are two ways to avoid them. You can go around them, or you can jump over them.

"My favorite courses are nasty, technical downhills that frighten my mom."

Josh Ivey, a downhill mountain-biking star by the time he was 15.

Technique

Riding downhill

These are some of the techniques off-road riders use for riding downhill quickly and safely.

Top tip!

Some off-road riders drop their saddle low for downhill riding. This keeps them from feeling as though they might be tipped over the handlebars.

1   Keep your arms and legs relaxed and slightly bent.

2   Keep looking as far ahead as possible. This makes it easier to relax and steer the bike.

3   When braking, move your weight back to keep the back wheel from lifting up.

4   On bumpy sections, stand up on the pedals. Your knees will absorb some of the bumps.

19

Cornering safely

Many riders who fall off their bikes do so on corners. They either lose their balance, or they crash into something they did not spot until it was too late.

High-speed cornering

Crashes on faster corners, such as when you are riding downhill, happen for two main reasons. The first is that the rider mistakes how tight the bend is, and runs off the road. The second is that they do not see a danger, such as a car sticking out of a side street, and crash into it.

It is easy to crash while riding around a corner.

Low-speed cornering

Most people who crash on low-speed corners do not slow down enough before they get to the corner. Trying to brake and go around a corner at the same time often leads to a crash.

Top tip!

The point where the two edges of a trail or road appear to meet in the distance is called the vanishing point. If it is getting closer, slow down. If it is getting further away, you can speed up.

Technique
Cornering practice

These are some of the techniques that good riders use to get round corners at higher speeds.

1 As you approach a corner, keep looking toward the vanishing point. Use it to adjust your speed.
2 Looking ahead also gives you a better chance of spotting dangers, such as parked cars, animals on the road, or sudden bends.
3 If you are not sure about your speed, slow down. You can always try it a little faster next time.
4 Try not to look at the ground in front of your wheel. If you look down, it starts to feel as if you are moving very fast. As a result, some riders tense up and fall off.

Bike tricks and BMX

BMX riders perform jumps and other tricks on their bikes. They ride on the street or in skate parks.

BMX bikes

BMX riders use bikes with tiny frames and small, 20-inch (50 cm) wheels. The wheels have pegs coming from the middle. These are short metal tubes for standing on. The bikes do not have gears and only have a front brake. BMX bikes are light and great for doing tricks but hard to ride long distances.

Skate-ramp riding

BMX riders use skate ramps to launch their tricks. Once the riders are in the air, they spin the bike around to land on the ramp. Some very skilled riders do stunts while they are in the air.

The best BMX riders can launch their bikes high into the air.

Street riding

Street riders leap and spin their bikes around in impressive tricks. BMX tricks include jumps, wheelies (riding along on the back wheel), and grinds (sliding the pegs along a piece of concrete or metal).

Technique

Learning to jump

Many BMX tricks start with a jump. Learning how to jump is an essential BMX skill.

1 Pedal so that you are traveling at a medium pace. Too slow makes it difficult to take off. Too fast is dangerous, at least at first.

2 Push down on the pedal at the same time as lifting the bars. The front wheel will lift into the air.

3 As the front wheel rises, slightly lean forward and push the handlebars forward and away from you. Keep a firm grip on them and the back wheel will come up into the air, too.

4 Either allow the wheels to land together or land the back wheel first. Ride away with a big grin on your face.

Health and fitness

Keeping healthy and fit makes cycling much easier. The hills will seem less steep, and it is easier to keep up with your friends.

Fuel for cycling

When you are cycling, your body is like an engine, powering the bike. The engine needs fuel. You get fuel from the food you eat.

When to eat

If you are only going to a friend's house or for a quick ride, you do not need to eat anything special. For longer rides, have something to eat an hour or two before you leave. This will ensure you have plenty of fuel in the tank. Good pre-ride foods include:

Keep taking little drinks of water or your legs will suddenly stop working.

- oatmeal
- pasta or rice

These have plenty of carbohydrates. Carbohydrates are foods that your body can quickly turn into energy.

Food to carry

It is a good idea to carry some food with you on longer rides, in case you need more energy. Bananas are great for this. They contain natural sugar, which gives your body a quick burst of energy.

Eating after a ride

After a long ride, you need to help your body recover from all the work it has done. Foods such as chicken or fish are great for this. They contain protein, which is a kind of food that helps your body grow and recover from injuries.

"Eat before you are hungry. Drink before you are thirsty. Rest before you are tired. Cover up before you are cold. Peel off before you are hot."

Paul de Vivie (also known as "Velocio"), famous French cyclist, pointing out how important it is to plan ahead for a bike ride.

Keeping fit

The best way to keep fit for cycling is to ride your bike. There are lots of other things you can also do to make cycling easier and more fun.

Warming up

People exercising need to warm up at the beginning. This means they need to get their muscles ready for hard work by doing some gentle work first. You can do this, too. Your warm-up could be stretching and bending, followed by gentle cycling.

Cycling training

One way to become more fit for cycling is to change your speed during your ride. Ride slowly, then sprint between landmarks such as trees or lamp posts. Then ride slower again before doing another sprint. Try this kind of riding with a group of friends.

"Ride lots."

Eddy Merckx, five times winner of the Tour de France and Italy, gives training advice.

Regular bike rides are a great way to stay fit and healthy.

Running builds up leg strength and fitness, which is good training for cyclists.

Other exercise

As well as cycling, there are plenty of other kinds of exercise that will help your cycling. Running builds up leg strength and breathing ability. Swimming also builds up breathing ability, and helps to strengthen your arms and shoulders. This might not sound important for cycling, but sprinters in particular use their shoulders to help with fast acceleration.

"It never gets easier, you just go faster."

Three-time Tour de France winner Greg LeMond.

Swimming improves your fitness which improves your cycling.

 **Top tip!**

The food you eat affects your fitness. Here are some foods that are good for your body, and some to avoid.

Yum! Yum!	Oh no!
Raw fruit	Chocolate and sweets
Rice or pasta	Fried potatoes
Steamed or raw vegetables	Cakes
Chicken or fish	Burgers

Biking around the world

These are some of the world's most famous cycling locations. Some of them, such as Mont Ventoux in France, attract cycling visitors from around the world.

Mountain thrills

Name Chamonix

Location France

Famous for Whether you are a mountain biker or a road rider, this area has some great thrills. Just make sure you like riding uphill—the town of Chamonix is right next to Mont Blanc, Europe's highest mountain!

Tough climb

Name Mont Ventoux

Location France

Famous for One of the toughest climbs in cycling. The best known route to the top climbs for 14 miles (22 km). The famous British cyclist Tommy Simpson died after racing to the top.

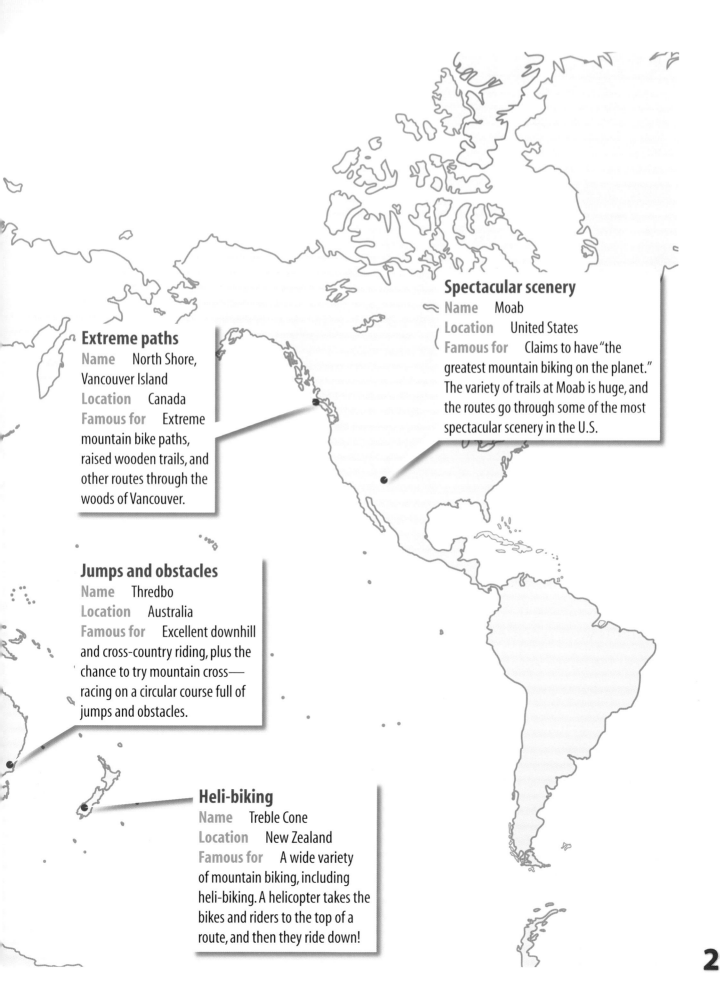

Extreme paths

Name North Shore, Vancouver Island
Location Canada
Famous for Extreme mountain bike paths, raised wooden trails, and other routes through the woods of Vancouver.

Spectacular scenery

Name Moab
Location United States
Famous for Claims to have "the greatest mountain biking on the planet." The variety of trails at Moab is huge, and the routes go through some of the most spectacular scenery in the U.S.

Jumps and obstacles

Name Thredbo
Location Australia
Famous for Excellent downhill and cross-country riding, plus the chance to try mountain cross—racing on a circular course full of jumps and obstacles.

Heli-biking

Name Treble Cone
Location New Zealand
Famous for A wide variety of mountain biking, including heli-biking. A helicopter takes the bikes and riders to the top of a route, and then they ride down!

Interview: Cycle crazy!

Louise has been cycling since she was two years old, or five if bikes with training wheels do not count. She rides both on and off-road.

How did you get into biking?
I lived a long way from school and I was always late. The only way I could get there on time was to cycle fast! I found that I really enjoyed it.

What is it you like about biking?
I like the freedom to go pretty much anywhere you like, plus the fact that you can get there quickly.

What is your favorite type of biking?
I think any type can be great fun, but off-road riding is probably my favorite.

What is your worst experience on a bike?
I had two flat tires, in the rain, and I was 12 miles (19 km) from the road. I'd forgotten my bike pump, so I had to walk. It was dark by the time I got home.

What are the best Web sites for cycling?
Ooh, tough one! I like www.singletrackworld.com for news of what's going on in Europe. The International Mountain Biking Association site is at www.imba.com.

Glossary

BMX
a single-gear bike with a low seat and higher handlebars, often used for doing tricks

brake pads
the soft, rubbery plastic that rubs against the wheel; this slows the bike when you pull on the brake levers

cranks
the pieces of metal to which the pedals are attached

forks
parts that join the front wheel to the frame of a bicycle

gears
mechanical system for changing the speed at which a cyclist has to pedal

gravity
the force that pulls objects down, toward the center of Earth

mountain bikes
bikes with strong frames, fat tires, and lots of gears that are used for off-road riding

off-road
on trails or paths where cars would not be able to drive

puncture
a hole in the tire that lets air out, making the tire flat

racers
a light bike with low, rounded handlebars, gears and thin wheels

suspension
something that absorbs bumps and shocks

Index